DICTIONARY WORDS

As you read this book, you will find that some words are darker black ink than others on the page. You should look up the meaning of these words in your dictionary, if you do not already know them.

OTHER TITLES IN THE SERIES

Based on William Shakespeare's

Romeo and Juliet

Stephen Waller
Series Editor Derek Strange

PENGUIN ENGLISH

PENGUIN ENGLISH

Published by the Penguin Group
Penguin Books Ltd, 27 Wrights Lane, London W8 5TZ, England
Penguin Books USA Inc., 375 Hudson Street, New York, New York 10014, USA
Penguin Books Australia Ltd, Ringwood, Victoria, Australia
Penguin Books Canada Ltd, 10 Alcorn Avenue, Toronto, Ontario, Canada M4V 3B2
Penguin Books (NZ) Ltd, 182–190 Wairau Road, Auckland 10, New Zealand

Penguin Books Ltd, Registered Offices: Harmondsworth, Middlesex, England

This adaptation published by Penguin Books in 1992
1 3 5 7 9 10 8 6 4 2

Text copyright © Stephen Waller, 1992
Illustrations copyright © Christian Birmingham, 1992
All rights reserved

The moral right of the adapter and illustrator has been asserted

Illustrations by Christian Birmingham

Printed in England by Clays Ltd, St Ives plc
Set in 11/14 pt Lasercomp Bembo

Romeo and Juliet

CHAPTER ONE

Is love a tender thing? it is too rough,
Too rude, too boisterous; and it pricks like thorn.

Act 1, Scene 4

The story had even reached the national papers.

*Liverpool's city centre was again the **scene** of violence late last night as young people fought in the streets. The trouble started soon after midnight when **youths** leaving Montague's nightclub in Main Parade met a group from a **rival** club, Capulet's. The police were called by angry neighbours. Two people were taken to hospital.*

*The **rivalry** between the two Liverpool clubs has led to fighting several times in recent months. At the same time there has been a violent war of words between the clubs' owners, Montague and Capulet. The two men are personal enemies. Each says that the other is trying to wreck his business. Following this latest trouble, local people want to see something done. Liverpool's Chief of Police said, 'I blame the owners. They must take responsibility. The young people simply follow their example. If this trouble doesn't stop, the clubs will have to close.'*

Montague was silent for a minute. He passed his hand through his thin grey hair, then handed the paper to his wife. She was sitting with her husband in the office at the back of the club in Main Parade.

'This has got to stop,' he said at last. 'I can't forgive Capulet, but I don't want to lose the club. We've put the best years of our lives into this place.'

Then, as if remembering that they were not alone, he

looked across the desk at the fair-haired young man standing patiently in front of him.

'Tell me how it started, Benvolio.'

The fair-haired boy started to explain. 'I did my best to stop it, Mr Montague,' he began. 'I was coming out of the club when I saw them fighting. I went and tried to calm things down. But then Capulet's nephew, Tybalt, appeared. He was looking for a fight as usual. Well, he started insulting us. He said he was going to teach us Montagues a lesson. Then he hit me, so I had to **defend** myself. After that, the police arrived. You know the rest.'

Montague nodded. His wife had read the newspaper report, but she was not interested in the details. She was thinking of her son.

'I'm just glad Romeo wasn't there yesterday,' she said. 'I don't know what I'd do if anything happened to him. Do you know where he is, Benvolio? I haven't seen him since yesterday lunchtime.'

'He was up very early this morning,' Benvolio replied. 'I saw him down by the docks, walking by himself. I called out to him, but he didn't turn round.'

Montague stood up and walked to the window. 'He seems to live in a world of his own these days. I don't know what's wrong with him. He won't talk to me about it.'

'I'm his friend,' said Benvolio. 'Let me try. He might talk to me. I think I know where to find him.' With these words Benvolio left the office.

◆

The playing fields were silent, and the lake shone in the clear morning light. Later, in the afternoon, children would come to sail boats and throw bread to the ducks. But now the only people in the park were a young woman and a little girl just old enough to walk. The mother was sitting on a seat in the sun while the girl played on the grass. The child's happy cries were the only sound.

Benvolio followed the path towards the bridge. He guessed that was where Romeo would be. He could suddenly see the bridge between the trees. Benvolio smiled. He had guessed correctly. A young man wearing jeans and a dark leather jacket was standing on the bridge, looking down at the water as if deep in thought. Benvolio called to his friend.

'Romeo! What are you doing here so early?'

The young man turned. 'Early? Is it?' He did not sound very pleased. 'Time seems to go so slowly. I don't know how I'm going to fill the hours until this evening.'

Benvolio joined him on the bridge. He looked at his friend without speaking. Romeo continued to look down at the water with lifeless eyes. For a moment Benvolio did not know what to say, then suddenly he smiled.

'I know what it is,' he said. 'You're in love! Don't try to deny it. I can see it.'

Romeo's face grew darker. 'In love? Out of love? What does it matter?'

'So I was right. What's her name?'

'Rosaline.' The name fell from Romeo's lips with a **sigh**.

'Rosaline?' Benvolio tried to hide his amusement. 'So you think she's pretty, do you?'

Romeo's eyes shone. 'Pretty? She's the most beautiful girl you've ever seen!' Then, in a quiet voice he added, 'But she's not interested in me.'

'Not interested in you? Have you asked her?'

'I don't have to,' answered Romeo angrily. 'I just know.'

Benvolio took his friend's arm. 'You shouldn't take things so seriously, Romeo. She's not the only girl around. If she doesn't want to know you, forget her! There are plenty of others as pretty as her. Or prettier!'

Romeo made a quick angry noise. 'There's no one like Rosaline!'

Benvolio was beginning to get tired of all this. 'You'll soon forget about her if you start looking around,' he said. 'You can't go on like this. You're behaving like a child.'

But Romeo refused to forget. 'So that's your advice? Well, thanks, but no thanks.'

'What do you mean?'

'I mean that I'm not the sort of person who forgets so easily.'

'What on earth's the matter with you, Romeo?' Benvolio cried. 'Have you gone completely mad?'

'Mad with love, yeah,' Romeo replied.

Benvolio laughed loudly. 'Look,' he suggested, 'I've got an idea. Rosaline often goes to Capulet's club, right?'

'That's right.'

'Well, there's a party at Capulet's tonight. She's sure to be there. Why don't we go? You'll be able to see Rosaline – and I'll be able to show you some other girls twice as pretty.'

Romeo looked doubtful, but Benvolio did not let him speak. 'There's nothing to worry about. There'll be so many people, nobody'll recognise us. How about it? Shall we go?'

'OK,' said Romeo after a pause, 'I'll come. But don't imagine I'm going to start running after the other girls. I'm only going to see Rosaline – and to show you that you're wrong.'

♦

'Of course I don't want the club to get a bad name,' Capulet said. 'I'm as worried about this as your uncle.' He seemed to be talking to himself as he walked across the living room and

Benvolio was beginning to get tired of this. 'You'll soon forget about her if you start looking around,' he said.

stood staring out at the garden. The roses were doing so well this year, but they gave him no pleasure today. After the trouble last night, his usual Sunday morning – with a late breakfast and then the papers – had been spoiled. The Sunday papers were lying unopened on the glass-topped coffee table. The Liverpool story was on the front page.

Paris nodded. He knew all about the rivalry between Capulet and Montague. His uncle, the Mayor of Liverpool, wanted Paris to be as successful in public life as him and, as well as introducing his nephew to all the most important people, he often spent hours discussing local **politics** with him.

'But you understand,' Capulet went on, 'I've never looked for trouble. Montague is responsible for all this as well as me.'

'It's a pity it's gone on for so long,' said Paris, 'but I hope that from now on you and Montague will be friends.' The fact was that he wanted to change the subject. 'You remember,' he began, 'we were talking about Juliet.'

Capulet smiled and sat down in an armchair. 'I'm sorry,' he said, 'you're right.' Then he became serious. 'Now don't misunderstand me,' he began. 'You say you want to marry Juliet. Well, it's good of you to come and ask me first. But, you know, she's very young. She hasn't seen much of life yet.'

Paris was quick to reply. 'She's old enough to know her own mind.'

Capulet went on. 'I didn't want her to grow up here in Liverpool. A nightclub is no place for a young girl. That's why I sent her away to school. She's the only thing that I care about in this world. I only want what's best for her.'

He looked at Paris thoughtfully, then said, 'But ask her yourself. It's her decision as well as mine, after all. Why don't you come to the club tonight? We're having a party. It's a thing we have every year around this time. All our friends are invited, and you're one of them. Juliet'll be there. She'll give you her answer.'

◆

'Mary, where's Juliet?'

The Capulets' old housekeeper was going into the dining room. Hearing Mrs Capulet's voice from the breakfast room, she looked round.

'I think she must be in her room, **madam**.'

'Can you ask her to come down, please. I want to talk to her.'

A minute later a good-looking girl of about sixteen appeared in the doorway. She was wearing a simple dress of blue cotton. Her thick brown hair fell loosely about her shoulders.

Mrs Capulet looked at her daughter with a proud smile. 'Well, Mary,' she said, 'what do you think? Juliet has turned into a real little lady since she was home last holidays.'

The housekeeper was delighted to give her opinion. 'Well, she always was the prettiest little thing I've ever seen,' she began. 'And I've watched her grow since she was a little baby. It seems like it was only yesterday I used to hold her in my arms and sing her to sleep.' The old woman paused. 'That was when my poor husband was still alive. He was a good man. You know, I remember one time, Juliet was playing in the park. She fell on her face in the grass, and my husband picked her up. "You fall on your face now, little lady," he said, laughing, "but you'll fall on your back when you're older. Isn't that right, Juliet?" And the child stopped crying and said, "Yes." Very serious, she was. I'll never forget it. "Isn't that right, Juliet?" he said. And the pretty child said "Yes." All serious.'

'Enough of that, Mary,' Mrs Capulet said, smiling.

But the housekeeper had not finished. 'Yes, madam. But I have to laugh when I think of it. "You'll fall on your back when you're older," he said. "Isn't that right?" And little Juliet said "Yes".'

'Oh, do stop it, Mary,' said Juliet impatiently.

'I won't say any more,' said the housekeeper, 'but I can't deny that you were the prettiest child I've ever seen. I hope I'll live long enough to see you married one day.'

Mrs Capulet turned to her daughter. 'Well, Juliet, that's just what I wanted to talk to you about. What do you feel about getting married?'

'The idea has never entered my head,' Juliet replied with a look of surprise.

'Well, you'd better start thinking about it now. Young Paris, the Mayor's nephew, wants to marry you. He's a very fine young man. One of the best families.'

'What a lovely young man!' the housekeeper added enthusiastically.

Mrs Capulet continued. 'Yes, he's good-looking, he's intelligent, and he's got money – a young man with a future. With his uncle's help, he'll go far. Just think! You'd be mixing with all the most important people. You won't find anyone better than him, I promise. He'll be at the party tonight, so be nice to him, won't you?'

Juliet did not want to disobey her mother. 'If he wants to talk to me, I'll talk to him,' she said coolly, 'but I can't promise any more than that.'

◆

Liverpool city centre was alive with young people, some grouped around shining motorbikes and their proud owners in leather jackets and boots, others laughing and calling to one another across the street. Small crowds were standing

'Young Paris, the Mayor's nephew, wants to marry you. He's a
very fine young man. One of the best families.'

outside popular pubs and discos, undecided whether to go in or stay outside and watch the street life. Romeo and Benvolio were on their way to the party at Capulet's with their friend, Mercutio. Benvolio and Mercutio were laughing and joking, but Romeo did not share their excitement.

'We can't wait to see *you* dance, Romeo,' said Mercutio with a sideways look at Benvolio.

'Not a hope,' answered Romeo, 'I'm just not in the right mood.'

'But you're in love,' laughed Mercutio. 'You're supposed to be happy.'

'You think love makes people happy?'

'Well, if it doesn't make you happy, why do you fall in love?'

'Why do birds sing? Why do policemen wear hats? Why does anybody do anything?'

'Why, why, why?' repeated Mercutio. 'That's three "whys". I'd be a "wise" man if I knew all the answers!'

'Only a fool asks questions like that,' Romeo replied quickly.

'Sometimes it's wiser to play the fool.'

'Come on, you two,' said Benvolio impatiently, 'we're wasting time.'

They walked faster along Main Parade towards Capulet's Club. There was already a crowd outside the entrance.

Romeo stopped. 'Are you sure this is a good idea?' he said. 'I had a dream last night.'

'So did I,' replied Mercutio quickly.

'What did you dream?' asked Romeo.

Mercutio smiled. 'I dreamed that dreams often tell lies.'

Benvolio laughed. 'Are you two going to stand there all night trying to be clever, or are we going in?'

But there was still a doubt in Romeo's mind. 'Something

tells me this isn't going to end well,' he thought to himself as they left the bright lights of the street and entered the club.

◆

It was hot inside, and the lights were low. The dance floor was a dark sea of bodies moving to the music. Around the edge of the floor young people were sitting at tables, following the dancers with their eyes. Whenever the music stopped for a moment, some left their tables and walked slowly onto the dance floor hand in hand. Others came back to their seats, their eyes shining.

Capulet was standing by the bar, a glass of whisky in his hand. With him was a short man of about the same age. 'I'm afraid our dancing days are over,' Capulet was saying. 'But we had some good times when we were younger, eh, Jack?'

'We did, too.'

Capulet was thinking back. 'How long is it since we last went dancing, I wonder?'

'A good thirty years,' his friend said.

'What! That long?' Capulet refused to believe it. 'It was at Lucentio's wedding, and that was about twenty-five years ago.'

'Twenty-five? More like thirty. His son's thirty, you know.'

Capulet was shocked. 'Thirty already? But he was only a schoolboy just a few years ago!'

Capulet shook his head slowly, and the two men laughed.

◆

'Who's that girl dancing with the tall fair-haired **guy**?'

Romeo pointed at a couple on the dance floor. The young barman did not know the girl's name. Romeo stood as if in a dream.

'Wow! She's beautiful,' he thought. 'The way she moves, the way she looks, the way she smiles. I must find out who she is. I'll wait until the music stops, then I'll go over and speak to her.' Then he smiled to himself. 'I thought I was in love before. What a fool! Now I know what beauty really is!'

Romeo was still looking at the girl on the dance floor when he realised that someone was standing in front of him. He looked up. A tall young man in a dark leather jacket was measuring him with his eyes. His face had an unpleasant look. He spoke angrily.

'I know you. You're a Montague, aren't you? What are you doing here? This is a Capulet party.'

Romeo recognised the face. It was Capulet's nephew, Tybalt. He tried to say something, but Tybalt went on in a voice full of hate.

'You're in trouble now, boy. I'm going to break every bone in your body. Your own parents won't recognise you when I've finished with you. Come on, let's go outside.'

Tybalt took hold of Romeo's arm and started to push him towards the exit. Then suddenly he stopped. His uncle, Capulet, had seen him and was coming towards them. Capulet looked at the two young men, then turned to Tybalt.

'What's going on, Tybalt? Has there been any trouble?'

Tybalt was still holding Romeo's arm. 'This is a Montague,' he said. 'He's got no business here. He's just come to insult us.'

Capulet turned to Romeo. His voice was friendly. 'You're young Romeo, aren't you?'

'Let me throw him out,' Tybalt cried impatiently.

'You take your hands off him,' said Capulet firmly. 'He hasn't done anything wrong. In fact, I've heard quite good things about him. I don't want any trouble in my club, so just leave him alone.

'You take your hands off him,' said Capulet firmly. 'He hasn't done anything wrong. I don't want any trouble in my club.'

And remember, this is a party. We're here to enjoy ourselves.'

'And I'm not going to let a Montague spoil it for us,' said Tybalt.

Capulet's voice was angry. 'You'll do what I say!' he said. 'Who do you think you are? You think you're going to start a fight here among the guests? Who's the boss around here, anyway, me or you? Now, I don't want to hear another word from you.'

But Tybalt refused to be quiet. 'This is an insult!' he complained.

Capulet could not believe his ears. 'What! You dare disobey me, do you? You'll be sorry for this! Just do what I tell you this minute.'

Tybalt's hand dropped from Romeo's arm and he was silent. But his eyes still burned. 'I'll let him go now,' he thought, 'but I won't forget this. This little adventure will cost him dearly.'

Romeo watched as Tybalt walked away. Capulet, too, had returned to his friends and was deep in conversation. Romeo was alone. His thoughts went back to the girl he had seen dancing. Where was she? Not on the dance floor any more. He looked round at the tables. For a moment he thought he had lost her. Then he saw her, sitting by herself at a table not far from him. Yes, he had been right – she was really beautiful, much more beautiful than any girl he had ever seen. He walked across to her table.

'Is it OK if I sit down?' he began.

The girl looked up and her eyes met his. She seemed surprised and looked at him for a moment without speaking.

'Of course,' she said at last.

'I saw you dancing,' said Romeo. 'I'd be happy to stand and watch you dancing all night. But I'd prefer to dance with you myself.'

The girl smiled. Then she held out her hand. 'Come on, then.'

Romeo took her hand and they walked onto the dance floor.

◆

When they returned to the table, the party was almost over. They had danced for over an hour, but they had lost all sense of time. Although they did not know each other's names, it was as if they had known each other all their lives. They laughed and looked at one another without a word, their faces suddenly serious. They kissed, and laughed again. Then another long kiss . . .

'Miss! Your mother wants to speak to you.'

It was the club doorman, sent to call Juliet to her mother. Juliet stood up quickly. She turned to Romeo and smiled before disappearing. Romeo was confused. He looked up at the doorman.

'Who's her mother?' he asked.

'Her mother is the wife of the owner of this place. Mrs Capulet. And whoever gets his hands on her daughter is a very lucky man! That's what I say!'

Romeo felt as if his heart had stopped. A Capulet! 'Is it possible?' he thought. 'How can life be so cruel?'

He was still sitting there when Benvolio found him.

'Let's go,' said Benvolio. 'It's getting late, and if we're not careful, we might get into trouble. Come on.'

Romeo did not understand a word of what Benvolio was saying. But he got up mechanically and followed him out of the club.

◆

When she came back to the table and found it empty, Juliet ran to the doorman.

'That guy I was talking to,' she said. 'Do you know his name?'

The doorman knew his name. 'That was Romeo,' he answered, 'Montague's son.'

Montague. The name her family hated most. 'I've fallen in love with a Montague!' she thought with sudden fear. 'How can he be a Montague? He seemed so gentle, so honest. He made me laugh, too.' She felt suddenly lost, confused.

CHAPTER TWO

O Romeo, Romeo! wherefore art thou Romeo?
Deny thy father, and refuse thy name;
Or if thou wilt not, be but sworn my love,
And I'll no longer be a Capulet.

Act 2, Scene 2

It was well past midnight and the street was empty – a street of big houses with double garages, and gardens with tall trees. There was very little traffic in this part of town during the day. Now there was none. All the houses were dark except one. Light still shone from the upstairs windows. The house stood in the middle of a large garden surrounded by a high wall. The dark shape of a man moved quickly down the street, along the wall, and stopped. He jumped, pulled himself up to the top of the wall and disappeared over it.

'Come on! We'll catch up with him.'

Benvolio ran across to the place where he had seen his friend disappear over the wall. Mercutio was not far behind him.

'Romeo! What are you doing?' called Benvolio.

'He's got more sense than us,' said Mercutio. 'He's gone home to bed.'

22

'But I saw him come down here and climb over into the garden of this house,' said Benvolio. 'You call him, Mercutio.'

Mercutio laughed. 'Hey, Romeo!' he shouted. 'Lover boy! Where are you? Just give us a sign so we know you're all right. A **sigh**, a line of a song, or something!'

They listened.

'Not a sound,' said Mercutio. 'He must be dead. Romeo! You can't run away like this. What about Rosaline? What about those beautiful eyes, those lips, that soft, little waist, those long legs, and all that . . .? Come back!'

Benvolio laughed. 'He won't like that!'

'Why should he be annoyed? I'm only asking him to think of his true love,' replied Mercutio.

But Benvolio was tired of waiting. 'He must be hiding in the garden,' he said. 'I don't know what's wrong with him. Let's go. If he wants to hide, that's his business.'

Mercutio agreed. 'Yeah. He's probably sitting under a tree in there, dreaming. I don't want to spend the night out here. I'm going home. See you.'

The two boys said goodnight and each went his own way home.

♦

Romeo stood listening until they had gone.

'It's all a big joke to them,' he thought. 'But what do they know about it?'

He looked around him. It was dark among the trees, but there was just enough light to see. He moved quickly across the garden' towards the house. What was he going to do? Why had he climbed into the garden? He did not know, but he felt sure that something would happen.

There was no sound from inside the house, but lights were

The window of one of the bedrooms was opened from inside and light fell onto the garden. Romeo stepped back into the shadow.

still on. Obviously Capulet had not yet gone to bed. He probably had not got back from the party until quite late. Suddenly Romeo froze. The window of one of the bedrooms was opened from inside and light fell onto the garden. Romeo stepped back into the shadow. Someone was standing at the window, looking out into the night. Could it be Juliet? Romeo held his breath. Yes, it was her! His heart began to work faster. He wanted to speak to her, but how? Juliet seemed to be thinking to herself. He wanted to know what she was thinking; he had to talk to her. But what was that? Had she said something?

'Ah . . .'

It was a gentle sound. A sigh. Romeo moved closer. Juliet was talking to the empty night sky, to herself.

'Romeo, Romeo, oh, why are you called Romeo?'

Romeo stood in the shadows, listening, unable to move.

'If you weren't called Romeo, then I could love you. Why can't you change your name? Or promise that you'll love me and I'll change mine.'

Romeo listened. Should he say something to her, he wondered? But she was speaking again.

'Names aren't that important, are they? What's a name? Nothing. A rose would still smell just as sweet if it had a different name. So, Romeo, throw away your name and take me in return!'

Romeo could not keep quiet any longer. He called up to the window.

'I'll stop being Romeo here and now if you like,' he cried.

Juliet was afraid. 'Who's there?' she asked.

'I can't tell you my name,' answered Romeo. 'You'd hate me if I did.'

Juliet gave a cry. 'I recognise that voice,' she said. 'You're Romeo, a Montague!'

Romeo came forward into the pool of light below Juliet's window.

'How did you get in?' Juliet asked. 'It's dangerous. If they find you, you'll be in serious trouble.'

'I climbed over the wall,' Romeo explained. 'But I'm not afraid of them. I'm more afraid of what you might say to me.'

But Juliet was worried. 'I don't want them to find you here.'

'They won't,' said Romeo. 'But if you're going to tell me to go away, perhaps it would be better if they did.'

'How did you find out where I live?' asked Juliet.

'It wasn't difficult. I just asked. I had to see you again.'

Juliet paused. 'You were listening. You heard everything I said, didn't you?' She seemed unsure of herself for a moment. 'Oh, how embarrassing! But it's too late now, isn't it? I've said it now.' Then, suddenly, 'Well, do you love me?'

But she did not wait for an answer. 'No, don't say anything! I know you'll say "Yes". And I'll probably believe you. But you'll laugh at me. This isn't a game for me, you know. If you do love me, Romeo, just say so honestly. Or perhaps you think I'm too easy. Would you prefer if I refused to speak to you, and made you chase around after me? But I can't hide my true feelings. Do you understand?'

Juliet stopped suddenly and neither of them spoke. Romeo did not know how to begin.

'Juliet,' he said at last, 'I promise you, and I hope to die if I tell a lie, that . . .'

But Juliet stopped him. 'Don't say that,' she said. 'People who talk like that never mean what they say.'

'But Juliet, I'm only trying to tell you . . .'

Juliet would not let him finish. 'No, wait,' she said. 'This is all wrong. It's too sudden. It's dangerous. Let's just leave it for tonight. We'll see each other again. Perhaps things will be different when we've had time to think.' She moved back inside the room. 'Good night, Romeo.'

Romeo called her back. 'Are you just going to leave me here, with nothing?'

'What do you want me to say?'

'Tell me you love me.'

'I told you that even before I knew you were listening. Though I'm sorry I said it now.'

'Why? Why are you sorry?' asked Romeo.

Juliet smiled. 'Because I wanted to tell you face to face, but now that you know, there's no point.'

There was a voice from inside the house. Juliet whispered. 'Don't go away. I'll be back in a minute.'

Romeo stood in the darkness, asking himself: Was this really happening? He was afraid that he would wake up suddenly and find it had all been a dream. It was too good to be true. But a moment later Juliet reappeared at the window.

'I can't talk any more now,' she said. 'But I *am* serious, Romeo. So if you really love me, then marry me. We'll have to do it secretly, of course; our families would never agree to it, would they? If you're serious, go and make the arrangements tomorrow. You can't phone me here and it's better that we're not seen together, so I'll send someone to you. If you're being honest with me, then I'm yours. Believe me.'

Again someone called to Juliet from inside the house.

'I'm coming,' she called. Then she turned back to Romeo. 'But if you're not serious,' she continued, 'just leave me alone. Don't ever come near me again. Good night.' And she disappeared.

Romeo could not think clearly. He did not know where to go. Home? But Juliet was here. Why go anywhere? Slowly he began to walk back through the garden towards the wall and the street. Then he heard Juliet's voice.

'Romeo! Psst! What? Have you gone already? Oh, Romeo!'

Romeo ran back to the house. 'I'm here,' he said.

'What time can I send someone . . . about the wedding?' she asked.

Romeo thought quickly. 'About ten,' he answered. 'Outside the Post Office in Queen Street.'

Juliet did not want to let him go. 'Ten o'clock? It's going to seem a very long time,' she said. 'But why did I call you back? I've forgotten!'

Romeo laughed. 'Well, I'll wait here until you remember.'

But Juliet looked at the sky. 'It's almost morning,' she said. 'You'd better go.'

'I'd prefer to stay here with you.'

'But you must go, my love. I'll say good night. Until tomorrow.'

'Sleep well,' said Romeo. Juliet had gone. 'Sleep well, Juliet,' he repeated to himself. 'And while you sleep, I'll go and see **Father** Laurence. He's known me since I was a child and has always been kind to me. He'll help us.'

◆

Father Laurence lived in a very different part of town where the houses were smaller and stood in long dark rows. They had been built for the families of the men that worked in the docks, but now that many ships had stopped coming to Liverpool, it was a poor, forgotten neighbourhood. Many of the people living there had no job, and young people grew up in the streets without love, without hope, and often in trouble with the police. Nobody seemed to care. That was why Laurence had chosen to live and work there. To the local people he was someone they knew really well, a true friend, not like other **priests**. He did not push himself on people – people came to him. And he never sent anyone away.

That Monday morning Father Laurence was working in his garden. As it was a public holiday and still very early, there was none of the usual Monday morning activity in the streets. Everything was quiet and peaceful. The old priest bent and inspected each plant carefully. It was an unusual garden, full of unusual plants. But he knew the name of each one.

'It's a strange thing,' he thought to himself, stopping to examine a broken leaf. 'Here's a plant which would look good in any garden. It has the most beautiful flowers – but it'll kill you if you eat its leaves. And here's another which most people would pull up and throw away. It doesn't look pretty, but it's used to make a valuable medicine. There are some plants here which are both things – poison and medicine.' He paused. 'It's like the good and the bad in our hearts.'

He was still thinking to himself when he heard a youthful voice.

'Good morning, Father!'

Romeo opened the gate and walked across the grass.

Father Laurence looked round in surprise.

'Romeo! What are you doing here so early? Couldn't you sleep? Is something wrong? Or . . . have you been up all night?'

'You guessed right, Father, I've been up all night,' said Romeo.

'God forgive you! Have you been with Rosaline?'

Romeo laughed. 'With Rosaline? Oh, no! I've forgotten all about her.'

'Well, that's good,' said Father Laurence. 'So where have you been?'

'At a party. At Capulet's.'

Father Laurence looked at Romeo sharply. 'Capulet's? There hasn't been any more trouble, has there?' he asked.

Romeo shook his head. 'No. Nothing like that, Father. No, the thing is, I met a girl last night.'

Father Laurence was beginning to understand. 'What about Rosaline?' he asked. 'I thought you were in love with her.'

Romeo shook his head again. 'That's finished. You always told me I ought to forget her.'

'But I didn't imagine you would fall in love again so soon!'

'Don't laugh at me, Father,' said Romeo in a serious voice. 'This girl is in love with me; Rosaline wasn't.'

'Well, aren't you going to tell me her name?'

Romeo paused. 'It's Juliet,' he said, 'Capulet's daughter.'

Father Laurence's face showed a mixture of surprise and disbelief.

'It's different this time,' Romeo continued. 'I talked to her last night after the party. She knows how I feel and she feels the same. We want to get married, Father.'

Father Laurence's mouth fell open. 'People don't get married just like that, Romeo! It's not like going into a shop and buying a loaf of bread!'

Romeo explained that he had thought it all over very carefully, that he knew what he was doing. The old priest listened, but he did not agree easily. He had seen too many unhappy, young married couples. And there was the added difficulty of the parents.

They talked for a long time until finally Laurence stopped and was silent for a minute or two, deep in thought.

'All right,' he said at last, 'I'll do it. I'll marry you and Juliet. Your two families have been enemies for years, but if you and Juliet marry, then they'll have to be friends, won't they? Maybe this wedding will help to end the trouble between them, and I'd be happy about that.'

♦

The weathermen had said that it was going to be hot, and they were right. Already by ten o'clock it was obvious that this was not a day for staying at home, and most people had taken advantage of the holiday to drive out of the city into the countryside or to the coast. In Queen Street all the shops were closed and the few people out walking looked bored and restless. Benvolio and Mercutio were looking for Romeo, but he was not at home, and his parents had not seen him since the day before. They had been to the park and down to the docks; they had looked into the Macdonalds on the corner of Parnell Street. But Romeo was nowhere to be found. Benvolio was getting worried.

'I hope nothing's happened. After last night, Tybalt'll be looking for him, too, I expect.'

'Looking for a fight, you mean,' said Mercutio.

'Romeo can look after himself.'

Mercutio laughed. 'Poor Romeo! If Rosaline can make him cry, I hate to think what Tybalt will do to him!'

'Why?' asked Benvolio. 'What's so special about Tybalt?'

'Tybalt? Tybalt's dangerous – really dangerous.'

They were walking past the Post Office when suddenly Benvolio pointed. 'Here's Romeo now.'

Mercutio was in a good mood. 'Romeo!' he called. 'Where the hell did you disappear to last night? We were looking for you all over the place.'

Romeo smiled. 'Sorry,' he said. 'Had something important to do.'

'More important than Rosaline?' joked Mercutio. 'You work fast!'

Benvolio was staring along the street, then he turned to his friends. 'Look!' he said. 'See that old woman? She seems to be coming over here. I think she wants to talk to us.'

They turned and saw Mary, the Capulet's housekeeper, hurrying towards them across the street, red-faced and breathing hard.

'God!' whispered Mercutio, pretending to be frightened. 'I've never seen anyone so ugly. I wonder if she's a **witch**!'

They watched, laughing to themselves, as the old woman tried to pass between two closely parked cars. She seemed to get stuck and was caught for a moment, waving her handbag helplessly in the air. When she eventually managed to free herself, she straightened her coat and came towards them. Romeo and Benvolio tried hard not to laugh out loud as Mercutio stepped forward.

'A very good morning to you,' he said with a pleasant smile. 'Can we help you look for it?'

The housekeeper looked at him sharply. 'What are you talking about? Look for what?'

'Your **broomstick**,' Mercutio went on with a serious face. 'You've lost your broomstick, haven't you?'

The housekeeper stared at the three of them angrily. 'I'm looking for a young man called Romeo,' she said. 'Do any of you know him?'

Romeo was about to answer, when Mercutio gave him a push. 'Romeo! Why didn't you tell us she was a friend of yours?'

Benvolio and Mercutio laughed loudly and walked away, leaving Romeo and the old woman alone.

'Who was that rude young man?' asked the housekeeper.

'Oh, just someone who likes the sound of his own voice. But he doesn't mean half of what he says.'

'Well, he'd better be careful with me. Nobody talks to me like that, no sir!'

They watched, laughing to themselves, as the old woman tried to pass between two closely parked cars.

Then she remembered Juliet's message. 'Now, young man,' she began, 'Juliet asked me to find you. I'm not going to tell you what she asked me to say, but I will say this to you: if your intentions with the girl are not honest, you'll be sorry! Just a friendly warning, you know . . .'

'I promise you . . .'

But she did not let him finish.

'Thank God,' said the housekeeper. 'I'll tell her. She'll be a happy woman.'

'What will you tell her?' asked Romeo. 'I haven't said anything.'

'I'll tell her that you promise. So you must be a real gentleman.'

Romeo laughed, then quickly became serious. 'Listen. Tell her to come to Father Laurence's church this afternoon. We'll be married there.'

'This afternoon? She'll be there.' The housekeeper laughed quietly to herself. 'You know, poor Juliet has been very worried. Paris, the Mayor's nephew, wants to marry her, but she hates the idea. I make her angry sometimes. I tell her that Paris is exactly the right husband for her. You should see her face!'

Romeo smiled. 'Tell Juliet I love her.'

'I will, young man, I will,' the housekeeper said as she turned to go.

◆

Juliet was waiting impatiently in the garden. It was nearly one o'clock, and the housekeeper had been gone for three hours.

'Why is she taking so long?' thought Juliet. 'Maybe she can't find him. No, that can't be it. She's just slow. She's too old to remember what it's like being in love.'

At that moment the housekeeper appeared at the front gate. Juliet ran to open it.

'Mary,' she cried, 'did you find him? What did he say?'

The housekeeper rested with her hand on Juliet's arm, breathing heavily.

'What's the matter, Mary?' asked Juliet. 'What's wrong? What did he say? Please tell me.'

The housekeeper sighed. 'Just let me sit down for a moment and get my breath back. I'm too old for this sort of thing, running round the place like this, you know.' She sat down on a seat by the garden wall. 'Ah! That's better! My poor old bones!'

'You can have my bones,' said Juliet impatiently, 'if you'll hurry up and give me your news. Now, tell me. What happened?'

'Can't you wait a second? Can't you see I'm out of breath?'

Juliet tried to stay calm. 'But you've got enough breath to tell me that you're out of breath! Is it good or bad news, just tell me that. Then I'll shut up.'

'Well, I must say he's not a bad-looking boy, your Romeo,' the housekeeper began. 'Have you had your lunch yet?'

'Lunch? No.' Juliet's voice got sharper. 'But why do you ask me that, Mary? What did Romeo say about our wedding?'

The housekeeper held her head. 'Ooh! My poor head,' she complained. 'I've got a terrible headache. And my back, too! And you're to blame for sending me out like this.'

Juliet took the old woman's hand and spoke more gently. 'I'm sorry, Mary. I really am. But please tell me what Romeo says.'

'He says –' the old woman began, 'where's your mother?'

'Indoors, I think. Why?' replied Juliet, jumping up, tears of impatience in her eyes. 'I don't understand why you can't just tell me?'

'Do you know Father Laurence's church down near the docks?'

'Yes.'

'Romeo'll be waiting for you there. Father Laurence will marry you this afternoon.' The housekeeper laughed. 'Why, Juliet, your face has gone all pink! But hurry up now. Off you go and get ready.'

♦

The church stood facing a garage, with a row of small shops on one side and an empty factory building on the other. Its grey walls had obviously not been cleaned for many years and one or two of the windows were broken. But the door was recently painted, and a notice by the gate pointed to a small side entrance, marked 'Youth Club'. Usually, this was a noisy street but today it was quiet. Romeo was standing with Father Laurence on the steps of the church.

'Let's hope that heaven's on our side,' the old priest was saying. 'We don't want this wedding to make things worse.'

Romeo agreed. 'But whatever happens,' he added, 'Juliet and I will be together.'

Father Laurence shook his head. 'That's not the point, Romeo. I don't know! When I hear you talk like that, I wonder why I'm doing this.'

'Don't worry, Father,' said Romeo. 'I know . . .'

'Worry?' Father Laurence took Romeo's arm. 'Of course I worry! Do you have any idea of what will happen when your parents find out about this? I just hope you've thought about it enough.'

He stopped suddenly. Juliet had arrived. She was hurrying along the street towards them.

'Here she comes,' said Laurence. 'What a lovely girl she is!'

'Good afternoon, Father,' said Juliet. She turned to Romeo.

Their arms went round each other and they held each other for a moment.

'Come with me,' said Laurence. 'This won't take long. You'll be husband and wife soon enough for all that.'

CHAPTER THREE

Lovers can see to do their amorous rites
By their own beauties.

Act 3, Scene 2

It was Monday afternoon and the usually crowded city centre was almost empty. A police car drove slowly along Henrietta Street and stopped on the corner of Denmark Place. Everything was quiet.

Benvolio and Mercutio were walking along Main Parade. They knew the café by the bus station was open and they needed something to drink. Benvolio sighed – it was hot.

'I don't think we should be walking around this part of town,' he said. 'What if we meet Tybalt and his friends? You know they often meet up near here.'

Mercutio laughed. 'What if we do? Don't tell me you don't like a good fight, Benvolio!'

'What do you mean?'

'Well, you're not the sort of person who likes to miss a good opportunity for a fight. You're always ready to hit anyone that dares even to look at you. Don't pretend that isn't true! Remember that time you had a fight with someone just because you didn't like the colour of his shoes! So now don't talk to me about keeping out of trouble!'

They walked on down the Parade. Suddenly Benvolio stopped. 'Well, now, look over there. Capulets.'

Mercutio looked. It was Tybalt. He was coming towards them, followed by three others. Mercutio buttoned up his leather jacket and waited. The Capulets came closer, then stopped and the two groups looked at each other in silence. Tybalt was the first to speak.

'I want to talk to you,' he said.

'Talk?' said Mercutio, looking straight at Tybalt. 'That all, is it? I was hoping for something a bit stronger than words.'

Tybalt took a step forward. They were face to face now. 'If you want a fight,' he said quietly, 'you can have one any time you like. But right now I'm looking for your friend, Romeo. Where is he?'

Mercutio made a sudden movement, but Benvolio held his arm.

'Not here,' Benvolio whispered. 'Too many people around.'

But Mercutio did not care. 'Let them watch,' he said.

At that moment Romeo appeared round the corner of Denmark Place, walking slowly and singing quietly to himself. Seeing the look on Benvolio's face, Tybalt turned and looked back along the Parade. Romeo had caught sight of his friends and was coming towards them. He did not seem to realise the danger. Tybalt turned his back on Mercutio and faced the newcomer.

'Here's the one I'm looking for,' he said.

Mercutio was angry, but Tybalt had forgotten him. There was a satisfied smile on Tybalt's lips, but when he spoke, his voice was cold and violent.

'You were lucky last night, Romeo,' he said. 'But you've got no one to look after you now, have you? And you're going to pay for that insult.'

Romeo saw that the Capulets had surrounded him. He tried to explain. 'Look, Tybalt,' he began, 'if you only knew, you wouldn't want a fight. We'd be friends. Believe me.'

But Tybalt was not interested. He was confident he had the advantage.

'Frightened then, are you?' he asked. 'Run if you want to, you chicken! But you won't get far.'

Mercutio could not control himself any longer. He took Tybalt by the shoulder and gave him a sudden push.

'Hit him, Romeo!' he shouted. 'What are you waiting for?'

Tybalt turned to Mercutio. 'What do you think you're doing, bird brain?' he asked.

Mercutio was hot with anger now. 'You think you're something special, don't you, Tybalt? Well, I'm going to show you you're not.'

He reached into his jacket and a knife appeared in his hand.

'Come on, then,' he said.

Tybalt looked hard at Mercutio. The next second there was a knife in his hand, too. For a moment the two young men circled each other, like angry cats, looking for a chance. Romeo was trying to pull Mercutio away when it happened. Tybalt jumped forward; there was a cry and Mercutio dropped to the ground with blood on his jacket. Tybalt turned and ran off along Main Parade towards the park, his friends following him. Benvolio and Romeo rushed to help their friend.

'Oh my God! Are you hurt?' asked Benvolio.

Mercutio's voice was broken. 'He knifed me. Get an ambulance.'

'It doesn't look serious,' said Romeo. 'You'll be all right.'

But he realised, as he said this, that it was already too late. Mercutio managed a smile.

'Sure. It's not serious. But it's enough. To hell with you Capulets and Montagues! He's killed me. If you hadn't pulled me back like that . . .! To hell with you all!' His head fell back.

Tybalt looked hard at Mercutio. The next second there was a knife in his hand, too.

Benvolio bent over him, then looked up at Romeo, his face white.

'He's dead.'

Romeo's mind was in a storm. His friend Mercutio was dead. Killed by Tybalt. And Tybalt was Juliet's cousin. Was this whole mess all because of him? What should he do? He thought of Juliet. Then he heard Benvolio's voice again.

'Look! It's Tybalt! He's coming back.'

Romeo looked round and saw Tybalt standing a few yards away.

'It's too late now,' he thought. 'What's done is done. He killed Mercutio, and I'm going to get him.'

Mercutio's knife was lying on the ground. Romeo picked it up and moved slowly towards Tybalt. Tybalt smiled. One or two people had stopped and were watching from a distance. Romeo threw himself at Tybalt and the two fell to the ground, their hands locked round each other's wrists. But Romeo was on top, and in a second he had broken Tybalt's hold on his wrist and had driven his knife deep into Tybalt's side. Tybalt coughed once, then was silent. Romeo stood up and looked around.

'Run!' said Benvolio wildly. 'For God's sake, don't just stand there. People are coming. The police'll get you. Get out of here!'

At last Romeo seemed to understand and ran away down the street. Benvolio was soon surrounded by a crowd of people.

◆

Liverpool was in the news again that evening and public opinion was angry. The names of the two clubs were on everybody's lips. They went together with other words like

'Run,' said Benvolio wildly. 'Don't just stand there. People are coming. The police'll get you. Get out of here!'

'violence', 'crime' and now 'murder'. The Police Chief was not pleased. He had called Montague and Capulet to his office and had spoken to them both personally for over an hour. There would be an **investigation** into the deaths, of course, but the Police Chief had no doubt that they were part of the continuing war between the two clubs and their owners. The fact that one of the two dead boys, Mercutio, was the son of a close friend of the Police Chief made everything worse.

Naturally, Capulet had tried to blame Romeo, although everybody knew that Tybalt had started the trouble. Obviously, Tybalt was Capulet's nephew, and Montague had not imagined that Capulet would be very forgiving. But Montague had done his best to make the Police Chief understand that Romeo was not a murderer. The police were searching for him now, and if they caught him, he would probably be found guilty and sent to prison. Ten or twelve years, if he was lucky. Probably more.

Montague's wife listened as her husband talked. His voice was slow and tired. His face was grey. Sitting in his chair behind the desk in his office, he seemed somehow smaller and older. She could not believe that this was really happening. Her son, Romeo, a murderer? The police searching for him? It was all like a bad dream.

◆

Juliet looked up at the clock on her bedroom wall for the twentieth time that evening. The hands of the clock had not moved. She looked out of the window at the garden in the clear evening light. She had been alone in her room all afternoon and the terrible news had not reached her.

'When will it be night,' she thought impatiently. 'I can't wait much longer. The hours are so long. Why can't it be night already? Then Romeo will come. Romeo, tonight we'll be together!'

There was a knock at the door. It was the housekeeper.

'Come in, Mary,' said Juliet.

Mary came slowly into the room and sat down heavily on the edge of the bed. She was crying. Juliet felt a sudden fear run through her body.

'Mary, what's wrong?' she cried.

'He's dead!' said the housekeeper. 'Dead! Killed!'

Juliet had to hold on to the cupboard to stop herself from falling.

'What are you saying?' she cried. 'He can't be!'

The housekeeper looked at Juliet, tears in her eyes. 'But it's true. And he did it.'

Juliet was confused. 'Are you trying to make it worse for me? Can't you just tell me what's happened? Do you mean Romeo has killed himself?'

But the housekeeper went on talking to herself. 'I saw the body. There was blood everywhere. His face was a horrible white.'

Juliet could not control her feelings. She threw herself onto the bed. Terrible thoughts rushed through her head. 'If he's dead, I don't want to go on living,' she thought. 'Let me die too.'

Then she realised the housekeeper was still talking.

'Tybalt!' Juliet heard her say, 'Dear Tybalt! He was a good boy. I never dreamed I would see him dead like that.'

Juliet sat up. 'What are you talking about?' she asked, shaking the old woman by the shoulder. 'Is Tybalt dead too? Tybalt and Romeo?'

The housekeeper shook her head. 'It's Tybalt that's dead and Romeo is wanted by the police. Romeo killed him.'

'Oh, God!' Juliet tried to understand. 'Romeo killed Tybalt? No!'

The housekeeper nodded. Suddenly the room seemed very cold. Was it possible? Romeo had done that? Juliet tried to think clearly. She had loved him. But he had murdered her cousin. So was this the real Romeo?

'Men are all the same. They're all liars and cheats,' the housekeeper said. 'You can't believe anything they say. Romeo? What a cheap little gangster!'

'Don't say that,' Juliet said angrily. 'You don't know him. He has nothing to be ashamed of. He's not a murderer. I know he's not. It's just not possible.'

The housekeeper turned to Juliet in surprise. 'You can't still love him after what he's done!'

'He's my husband,' replied Juliet quickly. She did not know what to think, but she was trying to make sense of what had happened. She guessed that Tybalt had probably started the fight. Romeo would never kill anyone unless he had no choice, she was sure of that. Maybe Tybalt had tried to kill him. A sudden feeling of guilt came over her. 'Why did I even think of blaming Romeo?' she thought sadly. He needed her now more than ever. 'But what can I do? He's wanted by the police. He'll have to live abroad for the rest of his life or go to prison. We'll never be happy together.' For a moment she lost all hope. 'It would be better if we were both dead!'

Juliet turned to the housekeeper. 'Where are my mother and father, Mary?'

'They've gone over to be with Tybalt's family. Everyone's very shocked. This is a terrible day for us all.'

'And I was looking forward to tonight – my wedding night,' said Juliet quietly. 'Now perhaps I'll never see him again.'

The housekeeper took Juliet's hand. 'I'll find him for you. He'll be here tonight. Don't worry. I think I know where to find him. He's probably hiding at Father Laurence's house.'

Juliet did not dare to hope. 'Oh, Mary,' she cried, 'if you can do it, I promise I'll never forget it. Look, here's a ring. Take it. Give it to Romeo. Tell him I'll be waiting for him here tonight. We'll say our last goodbye.'

◆

'Romeo!'

Father Laurence closed his front door and came into the front room. He called again.

'Romeo! It's me. There's no need to hide.'

Romeo appeared in the doorway.

'Father,' he said. 'What have you heard? What's going to happen to me?'

Laurence took Romeo by the arm and led him into the living room. They sat down. Laurence began to explain.

'The police are looking for you. You're wanted for murder.'

'I don't want to spend the rest of my life in prison,' said Romeo. 'It'd be better if Tybalt was still alive and I was dead.'

'Don't be a fool,' said Laurence. 'Remember, you're lucky. You're not dead. There's still hope.'

'What hope is there?' cried Romeo. 'I'll never see Juliet again. I'll be an old man before I get out of prison. Or do you think she'll come and visit me?'

Laurence almost smiled. 'Try to stay calm, Romeo,' he said. 'You won't help yourself by going on like that. Listen. I've been thinking. If the police catch you now, you haven't got much of a chance. The newspapers have already decided that you're a murderer, and they'll make sure that public opinion's against you. You won't be able to **defend** yourself; nobody will want to hear your side of the story. At the moment it looks like a simple murder, but we both know that it's not that simple. We have to try and show that you were caught up in something you couldn't control. It wasn't just you and Tybalt. It's the whole story of the war between your two families. I'm sure that we can build a strong argument in your **defence**. But we need time. If you could disappear for a few days, I'd have time to talk to some important people I know. I'll find a lawyer. This needs careful thought and preparation.'

Romeo had heard enough. 'This is what you call "hope"?' he cried. 'Run away? Leave Juliet? Hide? Then come back and give myself up to the police, go to prison, maybe not for twenty-five years, but for ten or fifteen? Is that the answer?' He stood up and walked angrily across the room, then turned. 'It's too late,' he said. 'There's no future for Juliet and me. Don't try to pretend.'

Laurence sighed. 'Be sensible, Romeo.'

Romeo's voice became more excited. 'You can't talk to me about something you don't understand! If you were young like me, if you loved Juliet, if you'd killed Tybalt and if you were wanted by the police, then I'd listen to you. But . . .'

Suddenly Romeo stopped. It was the doorbell.

'Quick,' said Laurence. 'Hide!'

Romeo did not move. 'I can't. It's too late.'

The doorbell rang again. Laurence pulled Romeo to his feet and pushed him towards the back room. 'They'll find you,' he said. 'In here. Quick!'

Again there was a ring at the door.

'All right! I'm coming.' Laurence turned to Romeo. 'Are you still here? What's the matter with you? Move!'

'Go to Juliet. She's waiting for you tonight. But don't stay too long.
Tomorrow you must go to London.'

Laurence went to the front door. 'Who's there?' he asked.

A voice from outside said, 'Let me in. Juliet sent me.'

Laurence opened the door and Mary, the old housekeeper, came in. She was out of breath.

'Father!' she began, 'where's Romeo? Is he here?'

'He is,' said Laurence, 'but I don't know what to do with him. He won't listen to me.'

The housekeeper was not surprised. 'Juliet's the same,' she said. 'She won't speak to anyone. She just lies on her bed crying.'

Romeo was listening from the next room. He came in.

'Mary! How is Juliet? Has she said anything? Does she think I'm an ordinary criminal, a murderer?'

The old woman turned to Romeo. 'She's locked herself in her room and hasn't stopped crying all evening. Sometimes I hear her call Tybalt's name, and then yours. "Romeo" she says and starts crying again.'

Romeo's eyes grew dark. ' "Romeo"? I hate the name! I've brought her nothing but trouble. Maybe it would be best if I killed myself.'

Laurence spoke quietly. 'This is no time for silly games, Romeo. In God's name, what do you think you're saying? You killed Tybalt and now you want to kill yourself? You should be ashamed of yourself. You've got so much, and you want to throw it all away? I thought you loved Juliet. Are you going to leave her now when she needs you most? Think for a moment how lucky you are. Juliet is alive. That's lucky. Tybalt wanted to kill you, but you killed him. That's lucky. The police are searching for you, but you're still free. That's lucky. You should be grateful, can't you see? Be careful, Romeo! People like you die unhappy.' He paused, then went on in a gentler voice. 'Go to Juliet. She's waiting for you tonight. But don't stay too long. Tomorrow you must go to London. Let me know where you're staying. And when we've had time to prepare everything, I'll send for you and you can come back.'

Laurence turned and spoke to the housekeeper. 'Go to Juliet. Tell her Romeo's coming.'

The old woman was grateful. She took the priest's hand. 'It's wonderful to hear you talk. You know just what to do!'

Romeo's voice was calmer as he said, 'Tell her I'll be there soon, Mary.'

The housekeeper suddenly remembered Juliet's message. 'Oh, yes! Here's something she asked me to give you,' she said, handing Romeo the ring. Then she hurried away.

Romeo turned to Laurence. 'I don't know how to thank you,' he began.

'Don't waste time,' said Laurence with a smile. 'It's late. I'll let you know how I get on. Now, goodnight. And take care.'

There were tears in Romeo's eyes as he pressed the old priest's hand. He was about to speak, but then he turned and left without a word.

◆

Capulet and his wife were tired. The police had called and they had had to answer more questions. They had spent several hours with Tybalt's parents. It had all been very difficult, and then, just as they were about to go to bed, Paris had arrived.

'With everything that's happened today,' Capulet was saying, 'we haven't had a chance to talk to Juliet. It's been terrible for her, too. She was very fond of Tybalt, you know. We all were. She won't come down tonight, I'm afraid. In fact, we'd all like to be in bed. It's very late.'

Paris stood up and started to apologise. 'I'm very sorry. I know this is not the best time to talk about getting married. I'll say goodnight. Please give my best wishes to Juliet.'

'I will,' said Mrs Capulet, standing up and hurrying to fetch the young man's coat. 'I'll talk to her tomorrow.'

Capulet put his hand on Paris's shoulder. The idea of his daughter marrying one of the richest young men in Liverpool had become fixed in his mind, and he was not prepared to let a small family problem spoil his plans.

'Look,' he said, 'I think I can safely say that Juliet will do what I tell her. In fact, I'm sure she will. My wife' – he looked quickly at his wife – 'my wife will go to her first thing tomorrow morning and tell her. . . . Let's see. Wednesday. . . . Erm, what day is it today?'

'Monday,' Paris replied.

'Monday? Well, perhaps Wednesday is too soon,' he laughed. 'Let's say Thursday. Tell her,' he said to his wife, 'she's going to get married to Paris on Thursday.' Then, turning to Paris: 'Is that soon enough? It won't be a big wedding, not after what's happened today. Just a few friends. But will that be OK?'

Paris was delighted. 'The sooner the better!'

'That's decided, then. Thursday it is.' Capulet shook Paris's hand. 'And now, if you'll excuse me, I'm going to bed. Goodnight.'

◆

'Do you have to go already? It's not morning yet.'

Juliet held Romeo's hand and tried to pull him back down onto the bed. But Romeo was already getting dressed.

'It'll be light soon,' he said. 'I can't stay any longer.'

Juliet looked out of the window. She could see the dark shapes of the trees against the sky.

'But that's just the street lights,' she said. 'There's no need for you to go yet.'

Romeo bent and kissed Juliet's face gently. 'I'll stay if you like. Let them find me. I'll believe you. I'll say it isn't morning yet.'

Juliet pushed him away and jumped up, her voice full of fear.

'It is!' she cried. 'It's almost light now. Quick. You must go.'

Suddenly they heard the housekeeper's voice at the bedroom door.

'Juliet!' she whispered. 'Your mother's coming.'

Juliet turned to Romeo. She was crying silently. 'I love you,' she said. 'Come back to me.'

With one last kiss Romeo climbed out of the window and down the wall into the garden. He had not yet reached the bottom when he heard Juliet's voice calling to him.

'Try to let me know how you are. I'll think of you all the time.'

Romeo promised. 'You'll hear from me.'

'Do you think we'll ever see each other again?'

Romeo's voice seemed to come from a great distance. 'I'm sure we will. And when we're old, we'll think back and all this will seem like a dream.'

Juliet watched as Romeo ran across the garden and disappeared over the wall. Then she turned and looked slowly around her room. She had never felt so completely alone.

There was a knock at the door.

'Juliet! Can I come in?'

It was her mother. She came and sat next to Juliet on the bed.

'Are you still crying over Tybalt? You know your tears won't bring him back!'

'I know,' answered Juliet, 'but you can't blame me for crying when I've lost a very dear friend.'

Mrs Capulet put her arm around Juliet's shoulders.

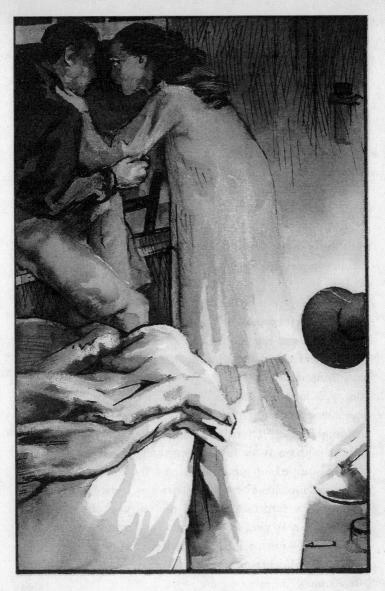

With one last kiss Romeo climbed out of the window and down the wall into the garden.

'When I think that that young murderer is still alive and free,' she began.

'What murderer?'

'Romeo, of course,' her mother replied.

Juliet did not answer. 'He may be a murderer,' she thought, 'but I hope he's far away by now. God will forgive him. I certainly do. Though no one has ever made me cry as much.'

'But don't worry,' her mother continued. 'They'll catch him and he'll be punished.'

'I won't be happy until I see Romeo,' cried Juliet, '– in prison.'

'You will,' said Mrs Capulet. 'But now, listen. I've got some good news.'

Juliet looked at her mother silently. Her mother began to explain.

'You know your father wants the best for you. Well, he's got a wonderful surprise for you.'

'What?' asked Juliet.

'Paris was here last night. He wanted to have a good talk with your father, about you. He's very much in love with you, you know – and he's serious. He wants to marry at once. Your father has agreed to make it all possible. The wedding'll be on Thursday at St Peter's church. Afterwards you can both go away, forget everything, just be together.'

Juliet jumped up and ran across the room. When she turned and looked at her mother, her eyes were shining.

'Is that the surprise? Well, let me tell you that I have no intention of marrying anybody, not on Thursday nor on any other day! You can tell my father I'm certainly not going to marry Paris. I'd prefer to marry Romeo – and you know I hate Romeo!'

Juliet's mother was not surprised, but she could hear her husband coming.

'Your father's coming now,' she said coldly. 'You can tell him yourself. But I'm warning you. He'll be very, very angry.'

Capulet entered the room followed by Mary, the house-keeper. Seeing Juliet's tears, he spoke impatiently.

'Still crying, girl? You'll make yourself ill if you're not careful.'

He turned to his wife. 'Well, did you tell her?'

'She says she's not going to marry Paris.'

Capulet looked from his wife to his daughter and back again.

'What?' he said slowly. 'She's not going to, did you say? I've found a rich, handsome young husband for her, and. . . Isn't Paris good enough for her? She should be grateful!' His voice was getting louder and louder.

Juliet tried to speak calmly. 'I *am* grateful, Father. I know you want the best for me, but. . .'

Capulet suddenly began to shout. 'You what! I didn't ask for your opinion, young lady! Don't give me any of your clever talk. Just you make sure you're ready to go to St Peter's church on Thursday or I'll pull you there by your hair! And now I don't want to hear another word from you!'

Mrs Capulet tried to calm her husband.

'Please,' cried Juliet, 'won't you just listen to me?'

But Capulet was too angry to listen. 'You'll obey me, girl,' he shouted. 'Either you marry Paris or I never want to see you in this house again! You can get out! And don't answer me back!'

The old housekeeper began to speak. 'You shouldn't shout at the poor girl like that, you know.'

Capulet turned quickly, his face red. 'You shut up!' he shouted angrily.

The housekeeper looked frightened. 'I was only trying to help,' she began.

'We don't need your help,' replied Capulet violently. 'Get out!'

'Aren't you being a bit hard on the girl?' his wife asked gently.

That only made Capulet more angry. 'Good God!' he shouted. 'I've worked my fingers to the bone to give her a good home. And now, when I've found a husband for her – a really good husband – this little fool tells me, "I'm not going to marry him." Well, if she doesn't want to marry Paris, she's not going to stay in this house. You think about that very carefully! And don't think I'm joking. I'm not. You can sleep in the streets and I won't lift a finger to help you, my girl.'

He turned and left the room. The door shut behind him with a crash. Juliet looked at her mother.

'Is that it?' she asked. 'Are you going to throw me out? Can't this marriage wait a week or two?'

But her mother looked away. 'Don't talk to me. You heard your father. You'll have to decide. I can't help you.'

With these words she followed her husband out of the room. Juliet was alone with the housekeeper. She took the old woman's hand.

'Mary! What can I do? You know I can't marry Paris. Please help me.'

The old woman was silent for a moment.

'I'll tell you what I think,' she said at last. 'Look at it this way. Romeo has gone and he can't come back. If he does, he'll go to prison. So you'll probably never see him again. What sort of marriage is that? I think the best thing would be to marry Paris. He's a real gentleman. What's Romeo compared to him? You'll be much happier with Paris, you know.'

Juliet's blood froze. 'Is that what you really think?' she asked.

'That's my honest opinion.'

'All right, then,' said Juliet. Her voice was cold and hard.

The housekeeper looked at her in surprise. 'What?'

'I was very foolish,' Juliet went on. 'Now I realise what I have to do. Please go and tell my parents that I'm sorry I made them angry. Tell them I've gone to see Father Laurence. I need to talk things over with him.'

The housekeeper was pleased. 'I'll tell them. And I'm sure you've made the right decision.'

The door closed and Juliet was alone.

'Heartless old woman!' she thought. 'How can anyone be so false? I'll never share any secrets with her again. But now I'd better hurry to see Father Laurence. Perhaps he can suggest something. And if he can't help, then I'll kill myself.'

CHAPTER FOUR

O! shut the door! and when thou hast done so,
Come weep with me; past hope, past cure, past help!

Act 4, Scene 1

Father Laurence tried to hide his confusion.

'On Thursday?' he repeated. 'This is very sudden.'

Paris explained that Capulet had decided the day for the wedding, and he, Paris, had not wanted to argue. That was why he had come to Laurence to discuss the arrangements.

But Laurence did not seem to share his enthusiasm. 'You say you haven't spoken to Juliet about it?' He shook his head unhappily. 'I don't like this.'

'She's been crying over the death of her cousin,' Paris

replied quickly. 'I haven't had a chance to talk to her. And her father thinks that this'll help her to forget.'

Laurence could not think of a reply. He stood by the window and looked out at the street. Someone was walking towards the house. It was Juliet. He turned to Paris.

'Look!' he said. 'Here comes Juliet.'

Laurence went to open the door. He quickly explained to Juliet that Paris was there. Paris stood up and went towards her as Juliet entered the room.

'Juliet! Are you ready for the big day?'

'I'll be ready when the big day arrives,' answered Juliet quietly.

'Thursday's the day,' Paris replied, smiling.

'What happens on Thursday is out of my control,' said Juliet. She turned to Father Laurence. 'Have you got a moment for me, Father?'

Laurence took Juliet's hand, but Paris continued.

'Have you come to open your heart to him, Juliet? If you have, don't deny to him that you love me.'

'I'll tell him I'm in love,' was Juliet's short answer.

'Until Thursday, then, Juliet. Goodbye.'

Paris kissed Juliet on the cheek, shook the priest's hand and left. Juliet felt weak. She sat down in a chair with her head in her hands. Tears ran down her face.

'It's hopeless,' she cried. 'There's no escape.'

Laurence sat next to her and put his arm around her. He did not know what to say.

'Juliet,' he began, 'Paris has told me everything. I hear your father wants you to marry him on Thursday, and that the wedding can't be delayed.'

'Don't say that, Father,' said Juliet. Her voice grew wilder and wilder. 'If you can't think of anything, I'll find a way. I belong to Romeo. You married us, remember. You've got to help me. I'll kill myself, I promise I will! Please! I mean what I say.'

'Wait!' said Laurence. His mind was working fast. Time was short and there was no easy answer. But one thing was certain: these two young people had come to him for help, and he was responsible for the situation. There had already been two deaths. It would be terrible if these two young people tried to kill themselves. Whatever happened, he must stop them doing that. God would never forgive him. He had to do something, even if it was against the law.

'There is a way,' he began slowly. 'But it's not an easy one. It would mean leaving everything behind and starting a new life in another country. But you say that you're ready to kill yourself if you have to marry Paris. If that's true, then I suppose you must be ready to try anything. I'll tell you what I have in mind.'

Juliet took the old priest's hand. 'Tell me,' she cried. 'Anything! I'll do anything!'

'Listen, then,' Laurence began. 'Go home. Tell your parents you'll marry Paris. Tomorrow is Wednesday. Well, when you go to bed tomorrow night, make sure that you're alone. Take this little bottle.'

Laurence went to a cupboard and came back with a small brown bottle.

'Take this bottle,' he went on, 'and drink the stuff in it. Don't worry. It won't hurt you. It's made from plants. You'll go to sleep, but it won't be an ordinary sleep. It'll be a very, very deep sleep. It'll seem as if you've stopped breathing, the blood will disappear from your face, your body will be stiff and cold. Everyone will think you're dead. You'll stay like that for twenty-four hours, then you'll wake up and be perfectly all right. On Thursday morning they'll find you and think you've killed yourself. You'll be put in a **coffin**

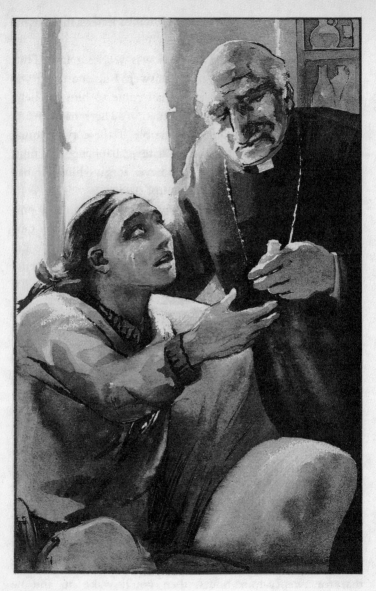

Julia did not stop to think for a moment. 'Give me the bottle.'
Father Laurence handed her the bottle and warned her to be careful.

and the coffin will be taken to St Peter's **chapel**. I'll send someone to tell Romeo about our plan and he'll come back to Liverpool. He and I will wait in the chapel until you wake up. Then you can escape with Romeo and leave the country. I think it could work.'

Juliet did not stop to think for a moment. 'Give me the bottle. Give it to me!'

Father Laurence handed her the bottle and warned her to be careful.

'I'll send a message to Romeo immediately,' he said. 'But now you'd better go. Be brave, Juliet, and don't lose hope. Everything will be all right. God be with you.'

◆

When Juliet arrived home, everyone was busy getting things ready for the wedding. She went straight to her father.

'Where have you been?' he asked coldly.

Juliet lowered her eyes. 'I've been to talk to Father Laurence. I realise now that I was wrong. I'm sorry. I've come to tell you I'll do what you say.'

'I'm glad to hear it,' Capulet said. 'I'll tell Paris.'

'I saw him at Laurence's house,' said Juliet quickly, 'and spoke to him myself.'

'Even better,' said Capulet. This was all very unusual. 'This Father Laurence is obviously a very sensible man. I'm very grateful to him.'

Juliet turned to the housekeeper. 'Mary, will you come upstairs and help me choose a dress for the wedding?'

When they had gone, Capulet congratulated himself. Everything was going to be just fine.

◆

It was late in the evening of the next day and Juliet was alone in her room. Yes, this was her room, those were her pictures on the walls, her nightdress hanging over the end of the bed. But she felt like a stranger. This had been her life up until now, but in a few hours she would say goodbye to it for ever. She could hear her parents talking downstairs and wondered if she would ever see them again. And Mary, the housekeeper? She had not spoken to her since the day before. Juliet went to her dressing table and picked up the little bottle that Father Laurence had given her. She held it in her hand and looked at it for a moment. She felt cold with fear.

'If this doesn't work,' she thought, 'what then? Will I have to marry Paris tomorrow?' A sudden doubt entered her mind. 'Perhaps it's a poison,' she thought. 'Perhaps Laurence wants to kill me so that no one will find out about Romeo and me. But that's impossible. He's a good man. I don't want to think that. But then, when they put me in the coffin, I might wake up before Romeo arrives and I won't be able to breathe. I'll go mad. What a horrible thought! I don't want to think about it.'

She walked to the window and breathed the sweet night air. The garden was peaceful in the moonlight.

'Romeo, my love,' she whispered to herself. 'This is our only hope.'

Taking the bottle, she raised it to her lips and drank. Almost immediately she began to feel sleepy. The room grew darker and she fell onto the bed.

♦

'Juliet! It's time to get up!'

Mary, the housekeeper, came into the room and opened the curtains. The room was filled with bright morning light.

'Still asleep?' she cried. 'On an important day like this! Come on, girl, wake up!'

She bent and shook Juliet gently. But Juliet did not move.

'You just wait until you're married to young Paris,' she laughed. 'You won't stay asleep then! Come on, now. Time to get up. Juliet!'

Juliet lay there without a sound. Suddenly the housekeeper was afraid. The girl's face was very white and still. Something was wrong.

'Juliet!' she shouted. 'Help! Juliet's dead! Help! Someone help me!'

There was the sound of feet running up the stairs. Mrs Capulet appeared in the doorway.

'What's all this shouting?' she asked.

The housekeeper pointed at the bed, unable to speak. In a moment the whole house was in confusion.

♦

'We don't know God's plans,' said Laurence. 'He's taken Juliet from you. We don't decide these things, you see. He does. But she's with Him now and she's happy there, I'm sure.'

Capulet was not listening. He sat with his head in his hands. He did not understand. The world did not make sense any more. Why was this happening to him? He began to talk to himself.

'She was everything to me – my only child,' he said. 'There's nothing left.'

Laurence shook his grey head sadly. 'We all have to die, you know. Juliet is at peace now, but we must go on living. There's work for us to do. We have to take her to the chapel of rest.'

Capulet held his hand over his eyes. 'This was going to be her wedding day,' he whispered. 'It was going to be such a happy day.'

CHAPTER FIVE

Where be these enemies? – Capulet! Montague!
See what a scourge is laid upon your hate.

Act 5, Scene 3

It is easy to disappear in a great city. London is a city of strangers, and the arrival of a young man from Liverpool is not noticed by anybody. Romeo had imagined that people would look at him, but he soon realised that here he was completely safe. On the first day he had met a young man from Glasgow who had offered him a place to stay. He was living with three others in a small house in a poorer part of the city. But Romeo spent most of his time walking restlessly around the streets.

That Thursday he was feeling confident. He had dreamt of Juliet. She was in his thoughts all the time. Early in the afternoon, he heard a knock on the door and jumped. Surely, it couldn't be the police? He stood behind the door and listened.

'Who's there?' he called.

'It's me – Balthasar!'

He immediately recognised the voice of one of his old schoolfriends. Quickly, he opened the door.

'Balthasar!' he cried. 'Good to see you. What's the news from Liverpool? How's Juliet? And my parents? Juliet first – how is she? As long as she's all right, everything's all right.'

Balthasar hung his head and did not look at Romeo.

'I don't know how to tell you this,' he began with difficulty. 'Juliet's all right, I suppose. She's not unhappy where she is now.' He paused, then in a quiet voice, 'She's dead, Romeo. I'm sorry. I. . . .'

He stopped. The look on Romeo's face was frightening.

'I . . . I don't know why she did it, Romeo. They found her this morning in her bed. It looks as if she killed herself. As soon as I heard about it, I came down here to tell you.'

Balthasar took his friend's arm, but Romeo did not seem to recognise him any more. His voice was as cold as ice.

'Do you know the time of the next train back to Liverpool?'

'You can't go back there now, Romeo!'

But Romeo was not interested in his friend's advice. 'You haven't heard from Father Laurence?'

Balthasar shook his head.

'Too bad,' said Romeo. 'Well, are you coming? Or am I going alone?'

Balthasar decided it was best not to argue. He followed Romeo towards the door. But Romeo stopped him.

'I've got something I want to do first,' he said. 'I'll meet you at the station.'

♦

A stranger can easily disappear in a city like London, but he can also find almost anything he wants there if he knows where to look for it. Once, when Romeo had gone to a pub with the others from the house, his Glasgow friend had pointed out one of the men drinking at the bar. 'That guy,' he had whispered into Romeo's ear, 'can get you anything you want. Special keys and things for opening locks, car number plates, false bank cards, you name it. Even guns.' Romeo had been shocked at the time, but now he tried to remember where that pub was. He hurried along empty back streets past rows of small houses with broken gates, dirty windows and gardens filled with rubbish. Finally, he found it. 'The Old Sun' it was called. He paused before going inside.

One or two of the men standing at the bar turned and

looked hard at him as he came in. They seemed ready to suspect any face they did not recognise. After a moment they returned to their beers and the stranger was forgotten. Romeo soon found the person he was looking for, sitting by himself in a corner, smoking a cigarette. He was a small man with a thin face and oily hair. He looked as if he had not shaved for days. Romeo sat down opposite him. The man gave Romeo a silent questioning look.

'You don't know me,' Romeo began. He was not sure how to explain his purpose. 'I need a gun,' he said in a low voice. 'Today. I've got money.'

The man did not move. His eyes were fixed on Romeo's eyes. He seemed to be trying to decide. His voice was quiet and cold when he spoke.

'Go away,' he said and began to read a newspaper that he took from the pocket of his dusty grey jacket. But he continued to look at Romeo out of the corner of his eye.

Romeo was not going to give in so easily. 'Tell me how much,' he went on. 'Say a price and I'll give you double.'

The man turned to Romeo. There was a look of doubt on his face. Neither of them spoke for a minute.

'Let's see the money,' the man said suddenly.

Romeo opened his jacket and showed him the notes.

'Come to the car park behind the cinema in about an hour,' the man said. 'Alone. And no tricks!'

An hour later Romeo was standing in the empty car park. He felt the notes in his pocket. What if the man came with some others, he thought? They could easily take the money from him and there would be nothing he could do. Then he laughed quietly to himself. Nothing mattered any more. He did not care.

'Private joke?'

Romeo jumped. The man was standing just behind him.

*Romeo gave him the notes, and the little man began to
count them.*

'Got the money, have you?'

Romeo gave him the notes, and the little man began to count them. He looked up at Romeo with an unpleasant smile.

'In trouble, are we? Well, this'll solve all your problems. But I've never seen you and you've never seen me. Right? Don't forget that!'

He handed Romeo a small packet, then turned his back and disappeared without another word. Romeo tore the packet open. The gun looked real. He checked. Yes, it had bullets, too. 'So there is honesty among criminals,' he thought. He put the gun into his pocket and looked at his watch. He had three quarters of an hour to get to the station.

♦

'Laurence?'

The voice at the other end of the telephone line sounded urgent. Father Laurence felt a sudden fear.

'It's me,' he replied. 'Who's that?'

'It's John,' the voice continued. 'I'm calling from London. Have you been out? I've been trying to get through to you all afternoon. Are you sure that number Romeo gave you is right? I rang several times yesterday, but there was no answer, not even later in the evening. There was still no answer this morning, so I thought I'd better go round there. I must've got there about two o'clock, but there was nobody there.'

'You mean you didn't give him my message?'

'How could I? I couldn't find him. I did my best.'

Laurence put the phone down. What would Romeo do if he heard that Juliet was dead? And Juliet, poor girl! It was already late in the evening. She would wake up soon. If he wasn't there to open the coffin, she might think he'd forgotten her. He had to hurry to the chapel.

♦

The chapel was hidden from the road by a high wall with bits of broken glass on top to stop people climbing over. Paris had managed to get the woman who cleaned the chapel to lend him the keys. As he came through the gate from the street, he switched on his **torch**. There was no moon, and the chapel was in complete darkness. The entrance was at the side, he remembered. He had been here earlier with Capulet and his wife, but now it was past midnight and there was nobody around. Paris's hand shook as he pushed the heavy door open and stepped inside the chapel. His shoes made a hollow sound on the stone floor. He knew the coffin was at the far end of the chapel, and began to move carefully in that direction between the rows of wooden seats. He was beginning to wonder: Why had he wanted to come back? What was he doing here in the middle of the night? Suddenly the coffin appeared in the light of his torch. He walked quickly towards it, then bent and examined the top. It was not nailed down. Carefully he opened the coffin. Juliet was lying there, her face calm and beautiful, her thick shining hair spread out on the pillow. She looked almost as if she was sleeping. Paris dropped onto his knees. Was he to blame for this, he wondered? But he had only wanted her to be happy. He had never imagined that she might actually kill herself.

Suddenly he heard a noise. Somebody was coming. He quickly switched off his torch and hid in a corner.

♦

When they reached the chapel, Romeo turned to Balthasar.

'Thanks for coming with me this far,' he said. 'But now, if you're my friend, you'll leave me and go home. I want to be alone.'

Balthasar was too frightened to argue, but he decided to hide not far away and wait. Romeo continued towards the chapel, pushed open the door and went inside. The tall windows appeared like grey shadows in the general darkness. As soon as he could see more clearly, he moved slowly forward between the seats. Suddenly he heard a man's voice.

'Montague!'

He froze. There was another person with him in the chapel. A dark shape was coming towards him.

'Murderer!' cried Paris. 'What are you doing here? You won't escape this time. I'll make sure of that. You'll get twenty-five years in prison.'

They were standing face to face now, though neither could see the other clearly. Paris stepped towards Romeo and took hold of his jacket. With a quick movement Romeo tore himself free.

'Don't be a fool,' said Romeo. 'Look. I don't want a fight with you. I'm giving you a chance to get out of here. But I warn you: don't get in my way!'

At that moment Paris hit him. Romeo fell backwards onto the stone floor. As he got back onto his feet, he felt the gun in his pocket. Perhaps if he saw the gun, Paris would leave him alone, he thought. But already Paris had taken hold of Romeo's arm and was bending it and bending it. . . . The sound of the shot in the small chapel was very loud.

'I warned you!' Romeo shouted.

Paris lay on the floor without moving. Romeo bent over him and examined his face.

'Paris!' he thought. 'Why didn't he just go away when I told him to?'

He could see the coffin now. It was open. She did not look any different. She was so beautiful! As beautiful as the day of their secret wedding. In his mind he saw her again climbing the steps of the church, that lovely smile on her lips. For a moment, then, everything had seemed possible, as if a dream had come true. But how quickly it had all been taken away from him! He bent and kissed Juliet's lips.

'Still warm?' he thought. 'Tybalt, Juliet, and now Paris. It's my turn now. I'd better finish this quickly.'

Romeo held the gun to his head.

♦

Laurence stopped and listened in fear. A second shot! What was happening? He ran towards the chapel, but his legs felt suddenly heavy. He was almost too frightened to enter. The torch shook in his hand.

The chapel seemed to be empty. There was the coffin. But – it was open! Laurence hurried forward. But what was that? Somebody was lying on the floor. He reached down and touched the man's jacket. His hand was sticky. Blood! He looked closer and recognised the face. It was Paris. And there was another body lying by the open coffin. Laurence tried to stay calm, but his hands were shaking. He bent over the second body. Romeo! How was it possible? Both dead, shot, killed!

Laurence turned to the coffin. Juliet had moved. She was waking up. He took her hand and her eyes opened. Seeing the old priest's face, she smiled and tried to sit up.

'I'm glad you're here,' she began. 'Where's Romeo?'

Laurence was frightened.

'Quick!' he whispered urgently. 'We've got to get out of here. Everything's gone wrong. Something terrible has happened. Romeo's here, but he's dead. Paris, too. Don't ask questions. There's no time. The police will be here in a minute. Come on! Quickly!'

He helped Juliet out of the coffin. Laurence's words were

Laurence bent over the second body. Romeo! How was it possible?
Both dead, shot, killed!

still in her ears, but what did they mean? She looked around and saw the two bodies lying on the stone floor. Slowly she began to realise – this was not some horrible dream. It was true. Her Romeo was dead.

'You go,' she said slowly. 'I'm staying here. Please! Go!'

Laurence looked at Juliet for a moment, then hurried out of the chapel without a word. Juliet fell on her knees by Romeo's body. There were no tears in her eyes. She had no feelings. It was over now and she wanted to die. She took the gun from Romeo's lifeless hand. There was noise outside. People were coming. She had to be quick.

'No time,' she thought. 'Why didn't you take me with you, Romeo?' Then looking at the gun, 'I hope this thing works.'

♦

The newspapers loved it, of course. Liverpool again. More trouble.

Young Lovers Die In Family Rivalry. Police Chief Orders Investigation.

The story was retold in a thousand different ways. It sounded unbelievable. A secret marriage, murders, **suicides**! According to the reports, the parents had been enemies for years. Now, of course, they were sorry. There was a photo of Montague and Capulet in each other's arms, their faces almost unrecognisable. There was a priest mixed up in it, too. He had said publicly that he was the guilty one. He had even asked to be punished! There were interviews with friends and family, neighbours and local people. Explanations! Everybody wanted explanations. But who would believe the true story?

ABOUT WILLIAM SHAKESPEARE

William Shakespeare (1564–1616) is England's greatest playwright and poet. He was born in Stratford-upon-Avon and went to London when he was a young man. There he became a successful actor and playwright, and later a part-owner of the famous Globe theatre. He wrote nearly forty plays, and most of them were seen by Queen Elizabeth I of England, and later, King James I. *Romeo and Juliet*, one of his early plays, was probably written in about 1595.

Shakespeare's plays are still popular, and they continue to be acted, in the theatre and on film, four hundred years after they were written. The famous musical *West Side Story* was based on *Romeo and Juliet*. The stories of the plays are both old and modern – they are about love, hate, jealousy, murder, revenge, greed, magic – and people in every century have found new enjoyment and new meaning in Shakespeare's works.

The Simply Shakespeare series retells the stories of the plays for today's world, keeping the names of Shakespeare's characters as a point of contact with the actual play. Other titles in the series are *Hamlet*, *Othello*, *King Lear* and *The Tempest*.

EXERCISES

Chapters One and Two: Who's who?

Look at this chart. It shows the relationship between one of the people in the story and other people. Who is the person in the middle?

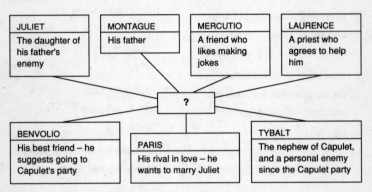

JULIET	MONTAGUE	MERCUTIO	LAURENCE
The daughter of his father's enemy	His father	A friend who likes making jokes	A priest who agrees to help him

?

BENVOLIO	PARIS	TYBALT
His best friend – he suggests going to Capulet's party	His rival in love – he wants to marry Juliet	The nephew of Capulet, and a personal enemy since the Capulet party

Now complete this chart.

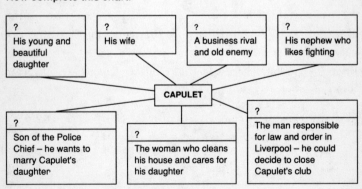

?	?	?	?
His young and beautiful daughter	His wife	A business rival and old enemy	His nephew who likes fighting

CAPULET

?	?	?
Son of the Police Chief – he wants to marry Capulet's daughter	The woman who cleans his house and cares for his daughter	The man responsible for law and order in Liverpool – he could decide to close Capulet's club

Now make a similar chart for Juliet.

Chapter Three

Match the questions on the left to the answers on the right.

1 Why is Tybalt looking for a fight with Romeo?

2 Why does Mercutio fight Tybalt?

3 Why does Father Laurence tell Romeo to go to London?

4 Why does Capulet get angry and warn Juliet that he will throw her out of the house?

5 Why does Juliet decide never to share her secrets with the housekeeper again?

a Because she refuses to marry Paris as her father wants her to.

b Because the housekeeper advises her to marry Paris, knowing that she is already married to Romeo.

c Because he feels that Romeo insulted him and his family by coming to their party.

d Because Laurence needs time to prepare a strong defence.

e Because he wants to defend Romeo and to teach Tybalt a lesson.

Chapters Four and Five

Put the sentences in the correct order to retell the story of what happens to Juliet and to Romeo. Write the numbers 1–6 in the boxes.

Juliet

☐ Juliet pretends to agree to marry Paris.

☐ Juliet finds Romeo dead and kills herself.

☐ Juliet goes to Father Laurence and asks for help.

☐ Juliet drinks Laurence's plant mixture.

☐ Juliet says goodbye to Romeo before he goes to London.

☐ Juliet wakes up in the coffin.

Romeo

☐ Romeo shoots himself.

☐ Laurence arrives at the chapel.

☐ Romeo buys a gun and re to Liverpool.

☐ Romeo hears that Juliet i dead.

☐ Romeo travels to London

☐ Paris and Romeo fight in chapel.

Discussion

1 Imagine the story ends differently. Romeo is caught by the police before he can kill himself. You now have to decide whether to send Romeo to prison and for how long. What are the arguments for and against? Is Romeo the only guilty person?

2 If Romeo and Juliet had not died, do you think they would have continued to love each other? Do we love the same people at sixteen as we do at thirty-five or fifty years old?

Writing

1 Stories like that of Romeo and Juliet offer journalists an opportunity to shock and entertain their readers. Imagine that you are a journalist who has to report the trouble in Liverpool. Write a newspaper story about Romeo and Juliet. Remember that your readers will want to know: a) what happened, b) how it happened and c) why it happened.

2 Father Laurence writes a letter to Romeo in London advising him on what he should do. Write the letter.

Review

Shakespeare wrote *Romeo and Juliet* nearly 400 years ago, but their names are still famous around the world today. Why is the story of these two young lovers so successful?